JOE DAVID BELLAMY

OLYMPIC

GOLD

MEDALIST

The North American
Review

Olympic Gold Medalist

ISBN 0-915996-03-0

L. C. Number: 78-73055

First Printing

Printed in the United States of America

ACKNOWLEDGMENTS
Grateful acknowledgment is made to the
editors and publishers of the following,
in which some of these poems appeared
originally: *A Review, Chariton Review,
The Cresset, Happiness Holding Tank,
Iowa Review, MidAtlantic Review, Ontario
Review, Open Places, Oyez Review, Paris
Review, Ploughshares, Poetry Northwest,
Poetry Now, Prairie Schooner, Quarterly
West,* and *Thicket;* and in the anthologies:
About the New Poetry, by Diane Wakoski,
University of Michigan Press; *On Turtle's
Back,* edited by Dennis Maloney, White
Pine Press; *Out of This World,* edited by
Gary and Judith Gildner, Iowa State
University Press; and *Seaway Valley Poets,*
edited by Stephen Gill and Roland C.
Hamel, Vesta Publications.

Photo credits: "Women" photo by Ralph
Gibson. Photos of Weeks Field, St.
Lawrence Univ., by Joe David Bellamy.

The North American Review
University of Northern Iowa
Cedar Falls, Iowa 50613

For my Father

Orin Ross Bellamy

(1908-1974)

Contents

Ancestors

8 Opening Up
10 17-Year Cicadas
12 Not Unlike the Runner
13 Newlyweds: Christmas, 1964
14 Iowa Stone Mason
15 For a Young English Setter
     Dead on His First Birthday
21 Heart Surgery

Weather

24 Spring Hits Upstate New York
26 A Talking Dog Is No Circus
27 Electrical Storm
28 Acres of Black Water
29 Marine Biology
30 Chastity and Death in Pennsylvania
31 The Yellow Velvet and Ultraviolet Humming
32 Solar Eclipse

Women

Plane Crashing over Boston   34

One Reader Writes   36

American Tourister Luggage   37

The Only Go-Go Girl in Las Vegas   38

The Muse Enters   40
Disguised as a Dental Assistant

Forties Movie Dream   41

Drilling for Oil   42

Wholesome Dreams of Winnetka   43

Swedish Cloudberry Liqueur   44

Lady Godiva Glides Like a Tiga   46

Olympic Gold Medalist

Curved Peripheries of Cinders and Space   48

The Weather Is Never the Same   49

Mile Run   50

You Would Have Made a Great Champion   51

Running My Heart Up   52

Racing through the Minefield   53

The Sniper   54

The Track at Weeks Field   55

Real Blood   56

Track Practice   57

The Heart Is Just a Pump   58

I Preserve My Father's Live Body   60

The Space around the Runner   61

Alone in the Gym I Can't Miss   62

The End of the Marathon   64

"Who can run the race with Death?"

—Samuel Johnson

Ancestors

Opening Up

"Breathe deeply now." Dr. Cooley fits the
black inhalation mask above my father's face the
chrome fittings, the varicolored tanks of oxygen, the
cyclopropane and nitrous oxide the
sweet cool mist the
mask's expensive rubber bends like soft leather my
father's body going limp   the
women's hands press needles into his hot arms the
white tape creases over locked in steel and blood they
are forcing something down his throat it
is a plastic crowbar quickly the
table expands

Cooley touches the knife to your chest
splits the skin going red
blade scraping bone
down the length of your body
Cooley receives the bone saw
thaaaaaa, thaaaaaaaaaap
wisps of blue smoke rise
moist dust powders the doctor's sleeve
as he strains, strains the
electric buzzing weakens, whines
your breast bone separates
from bottom to top

Cooley fits a retractor along the
raw edges of your ribcage
inch by inch
he opens this cavity
revealing 15,000 packs of Camels later the
slick mottled surfaces of your lungs

Now Cooley lifts the pink pericardial membrane
scissors it carefully open and
there like a dark fist
is your heart   its
scarred, irregular bulk
still undulating
still undulating

17-Year Cicadas

In 1956 it was a hot spring in
Cincinnati
We were in English class and the
17-year cicadas were
thumping against the windows

their boxy black thoraxes
quaint as old roadsters
their bright red eyes
their yellow wings veined like the
paired hinged seeds of maple trees

They live glorious short lives
wheeling above lilac bushes
crazy with singing and
mating in mid-air and
beating their heads against treetrunks
and boys pushing lawnmowers

That summer I was fourteen
I batted .363
I was no longer a virgin
I bounced one
off the wall in the
All-star game at Milford and
was out at third
on a muddy field

In orange track trunks
I cut swathe after swathe
around our yard
with a new green power mower
swatting and cursing
at the 17-year cicadas

They gathered in the rich air
in squadrons
thousands of cicadas
spiraling out of warm leaves drawn
by the roar of the mower
they dive-bombed me
overwhelmed me ricocheting
from my shoulders and legs
sticking to my back
coupling madly singing and
thunking on the mower housing

This year the 17-year cicadas are back
SEVENTEEN YEARS have passed

This is not a piece of fifties nostalgia
you understand
This is a poem about the patience
of insects
the deafening sound of their mating
the incredible whirr of their wings in the trees

Not Unlike the Runner

Our ancestors were farmers
they did their talking with their shoulder muscles
they got up at dawn and baked their brains
all day in forty-acre cornfields
they liked to listen to the singing of their bodies
blood set in motion, the hum of air
the virtues they most prized were
tenacity, endurance, raw physical energy
an unlimited capacity to absorb punishment
they could smell rain twenty miles away
they had the habit of gazing heavenward
as if what they most wanted to understand
would be coming from that direction and
what came never ceased to amaze them

Newlyweds: Christmas, 1964

for Connie

Asleep
your face toward the tree's fragrance
you can't see me
My own eyes
not so blue or large as yours
stare back to me
from the arc
of your silver barette

The pink sponge-curlers
in your nest of hair
are not so soft or ticklish
as the lobe of your ear

The mistletoe from Brown's
dangles clusters of berries
from the gently tinkling wind-chimes
Our Christmas pine has green lights
We bought a single white bulb
for twenty-two cents
to light the top

Iowa Stone Mason

for Sam

My infant son brings rocks into our house
he lugs enormous stones up from the creek
hordes them under his bed lines them up
At the beach too it is the rocks the stones
the rocks that interest him acres of rocks
he is kicking sorting bringing them home in
grocery sacks ruining his father's shocks

I ask him why he does this: "Because I
like to," says Sam, as if to say any fool
can see there is meaning in a rock.
There is not a doubt in his mind.
Tonight he is sleeping with a rock: "Love Rock,"
he calls it. He is five years old is Sam.

Sam's great grandfather (on his mother's
side) was an old Iowa stone mason.
I met him only once you had the sense
he knew how to hold on to things
wrenches hammer handles rocks crowbars
his tools were in perfect order he lived
in a solid stone house he built himself
Into his eighties he still had all his teeth
his hands were like great slabs of stone

For a Young English Setter
Dead on His First Birthday

*"From the best authorities on the
subject, it appears the English
Setter was a trained bird dog in
England approximately four hundred
years ago. . . ."*   —Davis Tuck

Great cast-iron doorwatcher
as you sit, head lifted
sifting fifty odors
out of the twilight,
motionless
except your quivering nose,
calloused strong-wristed dog's paws
pressed to the concrete,
forelegs locked at the elbows,
tense
with the ecstasy of such a feat

You were not meant for this world
of Sun Oil and Gainesburgers,
of Birds-Eye, Dow, and General Motors,
Exxon, Lucite, fiberglass,
mohair,
or eight-track stereophonic cartridges
Such talent
is
obsolete
You were not meant for

Your master the
jogger
clutching his watch,
bounding out the
back door,
yelling, "Let's go, old dog,"
tripping out over
each other's legs,
out the gate
around
across the front yard,
leaping the ditch,
breaking away
down the long road

You crash
through hedgerows
terrify startled sparrows
dodge
barbwire
head out over
lumpy earth, corn stubble
circle through
timothy, ragweed, wild wheat
Suddenly
the sproinng, sproinng of pheasant's wings
as if some hurtling stone is sprung
from a giant catapult

You never did catch me
with a gun in my hands,
a watch maybe,
but no other weapon.
Did it trouble you?

You *must* have had some memory.
Did you have any memory
in that knobby brow
of your birthplace
or the red barn
or the stall
where I plucked you
from your brothers
from your mother?
You were no runt then either.
You were the biggest in the litter.
You had the best head.

You ate us out of house and home
with your Alpo and Gravy-Train.
Ken-L-Ration wasn't good enough.
One aristocratic sniff was enough—
you would rather go hungry than eat
any vacuous packaged miracle.

You grew
on that diet,
Bird Dogge,
Shamelessly
packing our flower beds
with warm dog-turds,
your nose forever lifted, giddy
with the airy perfume
of the birds.

Then
the morning
(on my way to work)
I found you

lying
beside the road.
I stopped the car.
This is an odd place
to be sunning yourself,
I was going to say.
But I knew.
"You stupid dog," I said.
Your calloused paws
I dragged you
you were heavy
across the road
the ditch
at armslength
through weeds,
wanting to keep
my cuffs clean,
wanting not
to stretch my tie,
my polished shoes
beaded in the grass.
I was late.
My heart was pounding.
I shook my head at you.
I went inside and washed my hands.
"Connie," I said,
"I just found Beauregarde.
He was lying dead out beside the road."
"Oh my god," she said.

That afternoon
I brought the shovel.
I dragged you,
swarming with flies,

down near the lake.
There was a blue spruce there,
a low moist bed of weeds—
easy digging.
I chased and swatted flies
like a lunatic
and dug.
The digging was not so easy.
You were huge
in death.

That night in bed
I was afraid of you!
Of your being unearthed
by small animals,
coons and muskrats,
skunks, groundhogs,
weasels with rubbery fingers,
hyenas softly chuckling
as they dug, dug.
Hahahahahahaha!

I
who don't believe in ghosts
know I heard you
shaking water off your back,
vanishing
as a white streak
into the eye's periphery
for weeks.
Or your collar's jingling.

I made up with you.
I patted you and said:

"You're a good dog, Beauregarde.
I'm
sorry
for
everything
I've
done—
or
failed
to
do."
I
stroked your stiff ears.

Still
you worry me.
Why did you really . . .
why did you cross the road
that morning—
     sunlight splashing
     in the fields,
     birds, birds,
     alive and fragrant
     in the trees?
Was it suicide, old dog,
or just some impossible accident
in timing?

Heart Surgery

You do not
deserve this
someone
reaches in
and touches
your heart
touches
your actual
physical
heart breaks
the seal
of the body
and places
a hand   a
hand that
has been
just anywhere
or a piece of
cold steel
once merely
a rock that
has been
smelted and
beaten with
terrible
violence
at inhuman
temperatures
and may still
bear some
molecular
record some
memory or

aura of
its hideous
transformation
places this
blunt instrument
within your heart
within *your* heart
in its dark
airless chamber
your heart that
has never
experienced
daylight that
was magically
sealed
from the instant
of conception
within your
mother's womb
wrapped in
delicate tissues
coddled and groomed
and molded   gorged
with luscious
fluids
your earnest
and forever private
heart
set in
perfect motion
speeding through
the years to this
table
to this
intense
violation

Weather

Spring Hits Upstate New York

Overnight
the earth has
spit up or swallowed stones
the trees and houses have grown larger
a raw immensity of scale
bothers the eye's periphery and
odd earth smells
like menstruating rabbits and
crushed stalks of yellow grass or grain
like suppurating mudflats and
distant
puffs of seed floating in the
milky, watery air
(air like sunlight filtered
through a dusty screen)
crowd the nostrils

These trees are so still
cluttered with thin dead limbs
dark, rigid against the sky
like carcasses of extraterrestrial
insects in an ancient museum
The bark has thickened on these
shaggy beasts
they are impenetrable
on Arctic nights when
it is cold enough
to split stones
their gigantic paws
slowly moving
underground
like seacows

Embalmed now
they seem
brittle with age
in this heatwave
that warps tarpaper
on garage roofs
floods basements
excites birds
and cracks paint
on third floor ledges

A Talking Dog Is No Circus
for Lael

My Dalmatian yearns to speak to me this morning.
She is more-than-elegant in her sleek musculature—
demure, nubile, oddly cat-like before breakfast.
Once in the fields she crouches, her face to my face,
her eyes bulging with conviction, venerable
as the pocked statue of a griffin seated
two thousand years on the desert floor,
virgin throat pulsating with grisly secrets;
the beasts know how to live, I'm thinking,
blindly improvising beyond time—oh to be
drawn through life by such a nose!
The grasses dry to a sticky pertness
cantilevered toward the sun like radar dishes.
Man and dog, we curl up in this crisp orange light
my ear pressed desperately to her underbelly.
After hours of thundering, I hear:
Always pee on bushes at the *corners* of your yard
It's a dog-eat-dog world; only vomit on cloudy days
Avoid cats and porcupines; eat bloodroot for heartburn

Electrical Storm

Bridges and tramways are instantly stricken
electrical towers are twisted and buckle
the wet wind moans around lightning rods

The clouds will register seismic disturbances
tin roofs will burst open the lengths of their hinges
insulators will crack like hail on the sidewalks

Lightning flickers in the spaces between gables
splinters the wet sides of newly painted birdhouses
gutterspouts multiply like pieces of celery

The weathervane hums like a zither

Acres of Black Water

The lake pulses and swells
like a huge mushroom of black glass
rising towards us across the beach
as we sigh from our armchairs
losing ourselves
in the *New York Times*

The wind licks the water
our thumbprints quickly evaporate
a mountain of flat water
quivers
upon the porch railing
trembles at the posts
and parapets

Hours from now we undress
talking about the weather report
and the bark explodes
the water
topples and spreads: We go down
staring like lidless fishes at the
ancient trees towering above us

Marine Biology

"The sea is winning."
—Dr. Orrin Pilkey

My father, a Marine
two decades before
at Camp Lejeune
said the wind goes
right through you
in North Carolina
he knew something
about Marine biology

off blasting Japs with his trusty M-1 rifle
salvaging foggy tropical beaches
at five in the morning in
iron-hulled amphibious landing craft

Two decades later, I,
cutting up sharks in their trays the
scent of embalming fluid wafting out
along the icy sill, the Gothic casement
dreaming of Woods Hole and the sea,
could have found my own
life as a marine biologist

raking out netloads of sea creatures
stacking them quill to quill
or shoring up sandbags
with that Marine savoir-vivre
seeking beachheads of my own making

Chastity and Death in Pennsylvania

the blue wire
of fifty barbwire fences
hisses
in the mid-afternoon rain
in the distant woods
owls revolve
in their treetrunks

do her hands tingle
sliding in her skirt pockets
near such taut nylon?

imperceptibly
old apples are withering
on snow-touched branches

my daughter sleeping
this familiar creature—
I kiss her soft cheek

tires hissing, droning
snowflakes languidly falling—
another day gone

The Yellow Velvet and Ultraviolet Humming

Electrons humming in my cranium
bees that perform
unspeakable rites
hidden in the engorged lavender
translucent hearts
of every flower
swooning, tumescent, fatigued
the enormous canopy of air
the yellow velvet and ultraviolet humming, humming
the incredible architecture of desire

Soon they will die of heat
exhaustion, sunstroke, heart
failure
or whatever more loathsome disease
bees perish from
their bodies harden
their legs shrivel up
they blow along the roadway
amid pebbles and
clumps of dandelion fuzz
beercans, peanut shells, candy wrappers
powdered bones and hubcaps
their heady lives forgotten

Solar Eclipse

"I don't think the mind controls the body at all!
The heart controls the entire body just as the
sun controls the solar system."

—my father, after his second open heart operation

As a child I dreamed of a solar eclipse
the moon's immense shadow passing like the hand of God
across my shoulders and the yard
melting imperceptibly into the darkening willows—
a blond woman and I would have the entire planet
to ourselves and I would be . . . no longer a child
By the time this pact was sealed
the heavenly bodies would have swept on by
returning us to blissful daylight

On his deathbed my father dreamed the dream of Copernicus
His heart was the center of the solar system
The planets moved through their orbits in perfect sequence
the oceans rose and fell in their abject majesty
and suddenly the moon's eerie shadow passed
across the sod of the earth but it was not dark
and the gigantic wall of sun grew brighter and brighter
its aged scarred bulk was as white as bone
and its face was a clock without hands

Women

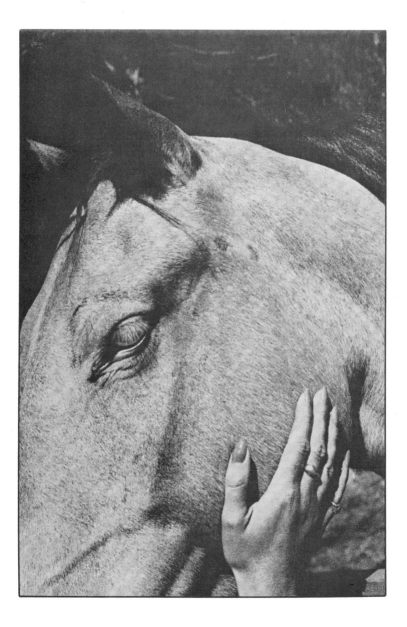

Plane Crashing over Boston

You are thinking of something else
the fuselage could crumple up like
a piece of wrinkled fruit
wrenched steel
engines working against each other
raaa, raaaa
the riveted wing-seam ripped open like
a giant zipper
falling you are
falling the cockpit
canopy blistered like a gourd
before the captain's eyes the
baggage compartment cracking
suitcases banging together
spilling silly women's hats
hairbrushes
bottles of shaving lotion
sailing through the sky
20,000 feet down
breaking like
eggs against rocks a
woman's slip dangling by one
strap from a treebranch like a
deflated parachute like
satin slipcovers like the
loosed pages of a
magazine fluttering slowly to the
ground like leaves a
red-haired stewardess trips and falls
against you
as the plane veers there is an
instant of pleasure a

bundle of fragrant hair passes along
your cheek one
breast beneath a
sheer white blouse
brushes your
shoulder and then the
deadly impact the
collapsing vertebrae the
neck snapped loose at the
medulla oblongata the
windows exploded the
mouthful of debris and the
siren-like whistling of the black winds of
chaos

One Reader Writes:

She would see it in *Time* magazine: a picture, himself in the foreground, still strapped to the seat, bent double across the belt, chin on chest, elbows limp, hands drooping and swollen, one shoeless foot two inches deep in muck, slightly deformed at the ankle, collar and cuffs amazingly spotless, a bolt from the tail-fin blown like a needle through his liver, blood and yellow bile oozing out through the stain on his suit, slowly filling the chromium ashtray in the armrest, cigarette butts rising to the top, overflowing; rust already setting in, melted plastic, pieces of burnt cloth, the ruined spirals of aluminum girders, lymph and ectoplasm flowing green in the mudpuddles, folded unused vomit bags stirring in the wind.

American Tourister Luggage

Here in the jungles of Guatemala
we are amused to find the
American Tourister Luggage farm
a gigantic airplane hangar
strung with clotheslines and
stretched, drying hides
curtains blowing out the windows
drawers full of studs and corners
rusty crowbars and lengths of wire
alligators of every shade
soaking in transparent vats. . . .
Where would you go with your
American Tourister Luggage
if we should meet in Istanbul?
You with your terrific complexion
Me with my trainload of skins

The Only Go-Go Girl in Las Vegas

She is the
only
go-go girl
in Las Vegas with a
white BMW
with a
chartreuse mohair bathrobe
with
dayglo pasties and
monogrammed underwear

She is the only go-go
girl in Las Vegas
with
an emerald-green Ferrari
with tulips in her fishtank
Dunhill in her humidor
onions in her glove compartment

She is the only go-go girl
in Nevada
who takes long leisurely walks
glistening with Baby Oil
in the desert in
a $90-dollar G-string
and an anklet
on Sunday afternoons

She can do the monkey
all   night   long

You should see her driving
hair flying
out your motel window
some April morning

She has the most amazing
rosebud garter on her
right thigh
She really shoves it to the
four-speed gearbox
She really shoves it
to the floor

The Muse Enters
Disguised as a Dental Assistant

The green glow of the dental lamp   the
top of a chimney and the top of a tree   are the
only tangible, though dreamlike, objects
to train your unfocussed eyes upon   when
this strange woman places her hands
into your mouth, and back   back
beneath your teeth in the tender recesses
beneath your tongue   where speech resides

Slowly   you find   you give in   the
frame   the arbitrary frame of the window
offers a solution to an elusive tradition
of metaphysics   while becoming simply
a painting of a chimney and a treetop   the
dental light reveals depth upon depth
of refracted glass, prismatic labyrinths
auroras to lose yourself in   as the
warm soft belly of the dental assistant
caresses your arm with such knowledgeable intimacy

Forties Movie Dream

a twin engine cranial transport
rustles
in the mirrored alcove
of the liberty ship with its
giant motors on board
terrific winches, cables turning
steam so thick it clots
the throat

twenty-nine reclining Wacs
zip up the backs of their
blue-and-white striped canvas
deckchairs
in the banshee breezes
off South Hyannis Port, Mass.

as the Wacs push their buttons
barrel staves rumble across gunmetal
depth charges sock the foam
yes suddenly the
higher frequencies are coming
unjammed
soundings, unheard of soundings
pour out
across the free ocean

Drilling for Oil

Lying here all day
tonguing each other's eardrums
pulling taffy
chewing jawbreakers
sliding through the sawdust on your wet behind
while the cracked water main in the cellar
already floods the first floor
there goes the stereo, my god
electrodes hissing, popping
the fireplace grate bites the head
off the chandelier. . . .
All day tomorrow I am seen holding my breath
lung-bright vacuum swelled to the breaking point
crouched near the floating endtable
and diving, diving with my diamond-tipped masonry bit
trying to drill another hole in the baseboard

Wholesome Dreams of Winnetka

Slanty-eyed woman, big-city girl
with your cigarettes like bullets
and your big black getaway car   the
kind of woman who makes grown men
beat holes in men's room walls
at Earl's Truck Haven on Route 80
just outside of Mishawaka   who
only moonlights as a CB trucker-whore
to gather copy for a porno flick
dreaming wholesome dreams of Winnetka
of Marlon Brando and Indiana autumn
and this errant underground life
Slanty-eyed woman, I'll wear your
Phi Beta Kappa key next to my heart

Swedish Cloudberry Liqueur

"And, if you travel north into glacier country,
you must experience Swedish Cloudberry Liqueur.
(It is possible to put 3,000-year-old ice into
your beverage which makes loud popping sounds
as it melts, releasing the ancient air that is
trapped inside.)" —from a Swedish travel folder

This ice
peed upon by reindeer
mashed by the dying feet of men   the
woolly mammoth frozen so fast
unchewed buttercups fell from his mouth
in the basement of the Smithsonian   the
Bog People—ancient sacrifices—hurled
into peat swamps their throats slit   the
brown muck congealing in their eyelids

For ten thousand sunny mornings
no sound echoes across this span of ice
then faintly distant sleighbells
muffled in the snow-clotted air
razor-thin runners crunching old
antelope bones brittle as toothpicks
in three seconds it is over crusts
of frozen water lock like steel around
pine branches   just here   the
footprint of an otter

Horned-helmeted Vikings busting their
swords against white rocks fighting
to the death with the jagged hilts inserting
their cold cocks into heavy-buttocked
blond women—their wives—out for a Sunday
stroll along the fjord: "Did you get a good
look at what's behind this tree, Brunhilde?
Thatagirl!" Throws her down on the glittering
snowbank rips off those pelt culottes buries
himself to the belly in her yellow muff

Lady Godiva Glides Like a Tiga

The horse comes clattering down Wellington Street
before Parliament
a huge white horse with diamonds in its ears
and big black horseshoes clanging
it is something like Diane Wakoski's horse (a nice horse)
only bigger   its balls are the size of avocados are
corded with black veins as they thump against its groin
once they raised a horse like this on pulleys
for the Russian queen as her mouth watered
its bulletproof hide is as soft as the fur of leopards
the horse thunders past the National Arts Centre
and down the hill by the Rideau Canal
where you are waiting under the bridge
like Brunhilde, like Lady Godiva and
you place your bare foot trembling into the stirrup and
you straddle this white monster you seize its mane and
thus begins your ride through the streets of that city

Olympic Gold Medalist

Curved Peripheries
of Cinders and Space

I rip my shirt off and start in
I keep tight in the inside lane
round the turn then break for
the center crease lugging the
curved peripheries of cinders and space
that balance the solar universe
the wind carrying me, the sun
splitting the bright sky
my lubricated knees flying, rising
gliding from time and place

The Weather Is Never the Same

Today the sky is endless   the
empty insubstantial bleachers
waver in the shimmering air   the
grass is browner   the sun
is foggier, distant, intense
my lungs are indifferent
they are not screaming

I think: last night behind   the
bleachers   a girl with long hair
lay down on the moist grass
with her lover   as
the air rustled in the trees
someone threw a beercan from
a red and white convertible
the girl cut her finger
on a strip of metal getting up
and held it to her lips
her tongue tasting of peppermint

Today at four o'clock
the sky was endless   a man
in orange track trunks
came through the gate
and started running
as he ran
he thought about the weather
the man was me

Mile Run

We are here at the Lincoln Relays. It is Cincinnati, Ohio, in 1957. The air is fragrant with wintergreen, which we rub on our legs layer after layer, and the distant smell of the Ford plant. There are runners from all over the city gathered in this grey concrete stadium. Some of them have shoes made of kangaroo skin and colors and stripes we have never seen before.

The black sprinters from Depores H. S. in their green warm-up suits and white shoes have a secret weapon. They chew grass before the race, real grass. They pull it up in the infield and trot around like chipmunks. They win every race this way. They are district champions.

When the loudspeaker calls us for the mile run, there is a skinny kid in the lane next to mine who shakes my hand foolishly and wishes me luck. My tongue is hot in my mouth. Somewhere from the bleachers, my father is watching. The gun fires like Mt. Vesuvius. We start running.

You Would Have Made
a Great Champion

the mystical ellipse
the crowd gathered there
as inexplicable in its way
as the great earthen snake
of the Ohio moundbuilders
or the pyramid of Cheops
stadia, stadia
eons of stadia and the
crowds always gathering
some day grass will grow
over this track as
it did at Thebes
as it did at Sparta
the sky will loom
high and white
like a blank page
like a bleached stone and
the surrounding edifice
deserted as it is now
will provide shelter
for snakes and termites
and not one sound
will be heard within
fifteen miles in any direction
except the soughing of the wind
through the rotting bleachers
and no one at all to hear it

Running My Heart Up

Running my heart up
letting the blood suck swoosh
through the veins, through the valves
keeping the veins elastic, smooth
hitting the flaps of cartilage, zap, zap
indispensable
like plastic
keeping the cartilage smooth, rubbery
keeping the blood aereated
keeping the aereated blood
full
of air
keeping the air
full
of breathing
keeping the blood-filled breath
full
of pumping
keeping the breathing
full
of air

Racing through the Minefield

The chain-link fence
around the track
is locked   as if
someone has decided
breathing   is
no longer allowed
Heart attacks and
dream deprivation
experiments
will now become
a way of life

Someone must take
a stand against
such   repression
something tells me
as I grip the steel
links hand over
hand   flip myself
over three strands
of crusted barbwire
drop to the ground
like a gigantic bird
and start sprinting
my heart exploding
with blood like a
four-barrel carburetor

The Sniper

Beads of rain in my hair
my shoes suck at the surface
the track is deserted . . . no
I see one car in the lot
there is a sniper in the car
a dark shape behind the
sweating windshield
each time I splash around
the long curve of cinders
he follows me along the barrel
through his scope-sight he is
leading me just so squeezing
the trigger the instant he fires
I drop on all fours
as if poleaxed
and press my belly to the ground
the bullet whizzes past my head
and shatters concrete or
barely grazes my left ear
here I come, my blond knees pumping
he is shooting now! now!
he is shooting now!

The Track at Weeks Field

The cinders pressed by thousands of feet
are turning to diamonds as we run
as we run we can see them changing
blinking among the helicoptered maple seeds
pressed like fossilized mushrooms into the dark
surface and the bits of dried grass blown
from the mowers and the
powdery black sun-baked mica

Our labor our immense cumulative labor
has no other monument than this
this debris
this amazing chemistry in slow-time
this wide ribbon of stones
this thoroughfare of well-tilled ashes

Real Blood

Today it is snowing . . . six inches deep already. . . .
I crunch out across the snow . . . cutting a jagged ellipse
of footprints where I believe the track to be. . . .
Out here there is blood on the snow!
Such a lot of blood—a dog must have cut its foot.
God, blood is bright on the snow. . . .
(We read about blood, but we seldom see it.)
Real blood. It is shocking. I think:
What does this mean? What does this blood mean?
I think about this blood as I run through the snow.
Surely this is some ancient message I can sense
but cannot name—some blood message. . . .
Someone was murdered here last night, I think.
(If the corpse is here, I don't want to find it.)
Someone's head was cut off and the body dragged away
behind the bleachers—*someone's bloody head was*
kicked around the football field at three A. M.
So slowly blood could be oozing out along my own sleeve
or from wounds on my feet—of course!
Blood could be bubbling through the holes in my track shoes.
It is so cold, my limbs are numb: is that it?
As I run, *I* am leaving trails of blood?

Track Practice

As I jog
track practice begins on the indoor tartan
young sprinters flick past my elbow like kangaroos
the coach emerges, watch in hand
                                    I imagine
how pleased my old coaches might be
that I am still out here at track practice
snow three-feet deep outside, a blizzard kicking up
Who else on those old teams would still be
out here twenty years later, putting in his laps?
ribbons and brittle striped shoes still in a trunk upstairs
                                    Some of them
were faster maybe but this proves
I was more dedicated.
"Clear the track!" someone yells. The coach stops me.
"Bellamy," he says. "You'll have to run somewhere else.
Sorry, but if we let you jog at track practice
we'd have to let everybody and his uncle do it.
Nothing personal, you understand."

The Heart Is Just a Pump

"Although the beating heart remains for some
a symbol of life and love, its role has been
put into perspective scientifically. The
brain is our master control; the heart is
just a pump."
                                        —Robert Glazer, M.D.

The heart is just a pump
a slab of wet meat
without eyes
merely a conduit of liquids

The heart is merely a muscle
its interests are limited
so many quarts per hour
the pleasures of contraction
pressure, heat, release
simple as a teakettle

The heart is also a time bomb
ticking away for years a dead
giveaway at airline checkpoints
risky to take aboard any vehicle
faster than an ordinary turtle

The heart has no emotions
to speak of—bland as a potato
chambered like a pomegranate
seedless, remote—

with tubes for ears
an adequate sense of rhythm
but a rotten sense of timing
like any fourth-rate rock musician

The heart is a selfish organ
it goes in for any cheap thrill
as long as it gets its kicks
sometimes it imagines itself
as a balloon floating
out over a deserted valley
or rolling along the ocean floor

Easily bored during middle age   the
heart often breaks through the chest wall
and hangs grotesquely by its own
blood vessels
like an old light fixture
unscrewed from the ceiling
suspended awkwardly by its wires

I Preserve My Father's Live Body

I preserve my father's live body within my body
Certain invisible waves sweep across the faces of continents

We are pinned together by antiseptic cotter pins
At the wrists and ankles and like ancient Christians
through the backs of our necks

I preserve my father's live body within my body
I sense this more at night when I am not awake
Certain chemical valences have no equivalents
Certain electrical connections do not diminish across space

They have reached in and violated my father's body hideously
Hideously the shockwaves move across the face of the planet
rattle and tear at the cotter pins
Certain invisible waves sweep across the faces of continents

His live body within my body is shrinking
Certain chemical valences have no equivalents

I preserve my father's live body within my body
I carry him like the body of a slaughtered animal
like a carcass in my grandmother's kitchen
Certain electrical connections distance does not effect

And the women are reaching in with their hands
Shaping their fingers to the configuration of split ribs
To remove his organs and place them in kettles of boiling water
Certain electrical connections do not diminish across space

Certain chemical valences have no equivalents

The Space around the Runner

The steady blur of green-red earth
as it passes like an orchard
The billowing concave of transparent air
as it passes like music
The distant energy of top-heavy wind-blown flowers
as it passes like fire
The perfect banked ellipse of bright cinders
as it passes like a halo
spinning, rising
taking its place beside Cassiopeia
in the chrono-synclastic infundibulum
of heaven

Alone in the Gym I Can't Miss

I play late at Augsbury gym
intramural games finish
crowds straggle off   until
the place is deserted
sixty thousand watts   the
whitest light
pours over my shoulders
as I drive spin release
the ball   the magic lap
of net calls back   the
rush of air   the soft
varnished boards cushion
my soles sinews flexing
rippling   the red suede
All-Stars darting beneath me
like small birds in a death
plunge to the sea

The
awesome canopy of space above
the incredible ceiling girders bolts
like clusters of nuggets
(Someone hung all that up there!)

Down here I am just as tremendous
Alone in the gym I can't miss
Think of the games I could win the
grace of my touch   the heart-rending
arc as the ball   the ball   the ball
as the ball   leaves my hand   my hand

Every pain in my life
was a preparation
for this great solo performance

The End of the Marathon

Here I come now
this feast of oxygen
the end of the marathon
the stadium in full view now
down the gravel runway
supporting the sun like an orange umbrella
the flags waving from its parapets
the TV dollies panning with me
the grinning cameramen
and the roar is starting, buoyant, incredible
all my blood is in my heart and limbs and lungs
my body rides free on a stream of blue air
at this speed
there is no strain to speak of
I stand still
and the earth moves
past me